LILIES WITHOUT

Laura Kasischke

AUSABLE PRESS

2007

Cover art: "View of the Moon" by John Adams Whipple, 1852
Courtesy of the Harvard College Library

Design and composition by Ausable Press
The type is Dante with Dante Titling.
Cover design by Rebecca Soderholm

Published by
AUSABLE PRESS
1026 HURRICANE ROAD, KEENE NY 12942
www.ausablepress.org

Distributed to the trade by:
Consortium Book Sales & Distribution
1045 Westgate Drive
Saint Paul, MN 55114-1065
(651) 221-9035
(651) 221-0124 (fax)
(800) 283-3572 (orders)

The acknowledgments appear on page 93 and constitute
a continuation of the copyrights page.

First Edition, 2007

Library of Congress Cataloging-in-Publication Data
Kasischke, Laura 1961—
Lilies without / Laura Kasischke.—1st American pbk.
p. cm.
ISBN 978-1-931337-36-6 (pbk. : alk. paper)
I. Title.

PS3561.A6993L55 2007
PS811'.54—dc22
2007027157

for Bill & Jack

They are neither finite quantities, or quantities infinitely small, nor yet nothing. May we not call them the ghosts of departed quantities?

—*George Berkeley on Newton's infinitesimals*

Had it lived long, it would have been
Lilies without, roses within.

—*Andrew Marvell, "The Nymph Complaining for the Death of her Fawn"*

LILIES WITHOUT

I.

II.

III.

I.

NEW DRESS

Dress of dreams and portents, worn

in memory, despite
the posted warnings
sunk deeply into the damp
sand
all along the shore. *(The green*

tragedy of the sea
about to happen to me.) Even

in my subconscious, I ignored them.
(The green

eternity of the sea, just around the corner.) That

whole ominous summer, I wore it, just
an intimation
then, a bit
of threatening ephemera. Another
rumor. Another
vicious whisper. And then
they sang. *(The giddy*

green
girls
of the sea.)

The feminine

maelstrom
of it, I wore. *(How*

quiet, at the edge of it, the riot. How

tiny, the police.) The *Sturm*

und Drang of it. The crypt
and mystery. The knife
in fog of it. The haunted
city of my enemy.
(And always
the green, floating, open
book of the sea.) That

dress, like

an era of deafness and imminent error, ending
even as I wore it, even as I dragged the damp

hem of it
everywhere
I wore it.

I AM THE COWARD WHO DID NOT
PICK UP THE PHONE

I am the coward who did not pick up the phone, so as never to know. So many clocks and yardsticks dumped into an ocean.

I am the ox which drew the cart full of urgent messages straight into the river, emerging none the wiser on the opposite side, never looking back at all those floating envelopes and post-cards, the wet ashes of some loved one's screams. How was I to know?

I am the warrior who killed the sparrow with a cannon. I am the guardian who led the child by the hand into the cloud, and emerged holding only an empty glove. O—

the digital ringing of it. The string of a kite of it, which I let go of. O, the commotion in the attic of it. In the front yard, in the back yard, in the driveway—all of which I heard nothing of, because I am the one who closed the windows and said, *This has nothing to do with us.*

In fact, I am the one singing this so loudly I cannot hear you even now. (Mama, what's happening outside? Honey, is that the phone?)

I am the one who sings:

The bones and shells of us.
The organic broth of us.
The Zen gong of us.
Oblivious, oblivious, oblivious.

MISS CONGENIALITY

There's a name given
after your death
and a name you must answer to while you're alive.

Like flowers, my friends—nodding, nodding. My
enemies, like space, drifting
away. They

praised my face, my enunciation, the power
I freely relinquished, and the fires

burning in the basements of my churches,
and the pendulums swinging
above my towers.
And my

heart (which was a Boy Scout

lost for years in a forest.) And my

soul (although the judges said
it weighed almost nothing
for goodness had devoured it.)

They praised my feet, the shoes
on my feet, my feet
on the floor, the floor—
and then

the sense of despair
I evoked with my smile, the song

I sang. The speech
I gave

about peace, in praise of the war. O,

they could not grant me the title I wanted

so they gave me the title I bore,

and stubbornly refused
to believe I was dead
long after my bloody mattress
had washed up on the shore.

TUESDAY

On Tuesday I catch a glimpse of him
around a corner
drinking his own shadow from a cup.

So this is it, the Future, huh? Just

a figure in a thin coat waiting for a bus?

From a passing car
I hear a song,

Boatman
Rowing, Rowing

Cargo full of screamers
But he keeps going

~

So why does he drop the cup
and run
when he sees I've seen him drinking from it? Why

this secret-agent stuff, this
big hush-hush? I'm
the mortal here, the mother, the one

with a bag of groceries, fumbling
with her keys at her car's trunk
on an ordinary Tuesday morning, song

on the radio, *Boatman, rowing. Just*
rowing. Boatman
rowing,

alone across an ocean

~

So suppose you were given a small
vial of sea,
and in it everything you needed
to create the world again, from scratch? Or

the First Seed? Or

the Original Plan? Or

the first song, *Knowing,*

knowing, weary of knowing, the boatman
hates his job,
but he keeps rowing

~

It's June. That boy
brought up blue
last summer from the bottom of the pool, he's

chasing a girl
this afternoon
with a black balloon. The earth

trembles beneath his tennis shoes. His mother

in the kitchen hums
a familiar tune, *Boatman*
rowing. Rowing. Boat

full of plans, but he keeps going

~

And if you were given a list of the names
of those who would die within the year—?

(Pearls
and coins
falling from the sky. A loaf
of bread that bled when it was cut with a knife.)

No, you would ask
for the list of those who'd fall

in love, instead, those

who would be born, get rich. You

would ask to be a child
at Disney World again—a frantic

child, still,
an abandoned child,
yes, but

a child nonetheless,

lost, happily, in a land of dreamy kitsch, and a chorus
of cartoon animals singing
a song your mother used to sing
in the car as you wept:

Rowing. Whiners. But I keep going . . .
If you two back there won't be quiet . . .

~

Outside
all night in the dark
a man kept calling to his dog. (The earth's

tides, the motion
of the planets, everything
nudging everything
else.) So,

when the phone rings in the morning
I already know
it will be that recording. *Rowing,*

rowing

~

And out the window, there it is,
the neighbor's dog, pawing

frantically at a rabbit hole—a hole
which whispers, *We*

are gone, all of us,
like so many Mondays,

but the dog keeps pawing.

TERRIBLE WORDS

I've said these words before, exactly these.

I said them in winter, in the car, at night,
warmed by the cigarette lighter's dangerous eye.

I said them in summer
when the flowers were in bloom
but there were too many biting flies to go outside.

Truly, I

was the first to say them. I was
their mouthpiece, their translator. On

the park bench in spring, these
words blew through me
like a few loose
tissues on the breeze. And then, in autumn,
the blossoms of them

hardened into fruit, which
fell disastrously out of the trees. And tonight—

Tonight they are birds
which have blown back to me,
and their wings in the air being beaten make
only the sound of a mountain
of books
slipping swiftly into the sea.

MY GRANDFATHER'S HEART

After he died, my grandfather's heart
became what it always had been:

a quiet woman
whose name was wood.

Last Sunday, in a church, I had
a clear vision of this. Lost now. What
Lot's wife saw before the salt—

Innumerable others.
Cities made of glass, like human health. *They
were still making love in their graves.*

Leather bats
dangled from the branches,
although the peaches were still green,
and the trucks hauled their cargoes
of hours down to the sea
while the gulls screamed over

those gold afternoons, which he

spent in a chair, not dreaming, but listening
to the neighbor's telephone
in a patch of sunlight ringing:

"Mrs. Wood? Mrs. Wood? Are you there?"

FASHION VICTIM

Too much mist to see the mountain. The freeway
lost in fog. The garden—a mirage. I order clothes
all day from catalogues—(a bird

flies into a cloud
and never flies back out)—like

a passenger on a doomed flight, raising
her glass in a toast
to the pilot, to the sky. They arrive

in long white boxes and in whispers
on the porch, like winter. Soon

there will be nothing but obscurity
as far as the eye can see. Until

there's only one leaf left

clinging to one tree. Until, like

my father over there in his chair, my
clothes are how you know it's me.

NEW DRESS (2)

Don't bury me in this
dress, my mother said.

She hung it from a knob
on a cupboard in the kitchen,
and sighed, and we
could all see why:

The ambition of it was stunning.

And it continued to stun us

all through dinner
and into dessert,

while, behind it, in the cupboard, the weevils
slept in the flour, as if

the whiteness and suffocating dust
in which they slept *(that*

weatherless, borderless place without
history, without bleeding, without

needing to scream, or eat, or breathe—no

rain, no taste, no pleading, no fuss) as if

it were a dream,
not a shroud,

just like the rest of us.

MISS JANUARY

On Friday, I fell—wearing

boots without treads, fell
from the great stupid height of myself. The boots

of a girl in a magazine, in a blizzard, on me. Or

you might say *I leapt*

from the cliff of myself,

while across the road a farmer
making peace with emptiness in a field
called out to me, and

my son, amused
and afraid at the same time, asked, *Mom,
are you okay?*

Of course, I was fine.
Bemirrored, the sky,
and

below me, below

the snow
and the dirt
and the seeds

of the pre-
Columbian flowers
asleep in the ground,
I could hear her clearly:

A woman
in sturdy shoes,

with a broad back (my
new paragon, my

ideal) walking,
steadily, chained
to a wheel.

MAY

Kindergarten. There was

a cherry-tree planted outside the classroom, a little brass plaque

in dirt. In
May, it shrieked into blossom, and I thought *"We've*

planted this tree in his memory" meant

that although this child who'd come before us
had already been dead for years, there

was still somehow a final tree
they'd managed to place
forever in his head.

In May, it burst into pastel
flames, or the tips of the fingers of a resurrected child: 1947-1953,
We've

planted this tree
in his memory.

O, what would it be like, I wondered then,

to have that thing explode
each year for a week into blossom in your head

so long after you were dead?

And now,
each May, when I
close my eyes, and see
all of them again

file out of darkness

in their black clothes

into sun poured all over a parking lot radiant with chrome, like

a branch of involuntary, perennial, screaming
light in my memory, I know.

LUNG

Once, a woman lay her head on a pillow to sleep without noticing that the pillow on which she lay her head was the tumorous, removed, left lung of her mother—

"In general, we are all in such a hurry these days. No one notices the things that matter, just under the surface, not even hidden, the waiting things. Be afraid. The tiny flying angels above the parking lot, just as you start your car—"

She had a dream of windows opening and closing. An unbearable beautiful organ bloating Mozart's Requiem in a forest. A man in a black suit sitting in an airport. Sitting on his suitcase. The suitcase full of air and flying buttresses attached to nothing, but holding aloft all the breath and loss of the public forum.

"Slow down. Now, you've driven straight through your own hometown. All of it changed. The debt birds screaming over the gravestone: 'You owe! You owe!'"

The woman asleep with her head on a lung awoke wondering in which jar she'd stored the small blank scrolls, the bees, the locks of the dead woman's hair. It wasn't yet morning. Her own heartbeat sounded to her as if someone were rhythmically shoveling hydrogen onto the stars. Inside the lung she heard a little voice singing a familiar song, but the lyrics had changed, *And the days . . .*

became too short to complete the tasks of the days,
And the nights too brief for sleep.
We exit this world the way we came,
Packing our blood-bundles one by one,
and stepping out of our bodies piece by piece.

POEM ENDING IN LINES FROM JARRELL

This morning, a dead mouse
under the kitchen counter. It had

a postcard of the cosmos in its eye. I was trying,

simply, to take the garbage out, but

screamed when I saw it and slammed the cupboard shut.

By noon, the light
in the living room
is irrationally bright. The candy dish is full
of small, hard pleasures. I live

in a quiet suburb. The jets

make childish sounds
in the sky. My

book on the couch is a bird in a pond
pushing itself somewhere with one bent wing . . . but I've

seen snapshots of my own child, wide-eyed, with his

whole life before him, a pinprick

of light in his eye
like an exquisite diamond viewed
from a dizzying height.

And I've been blinded by it:

If only you knew there was something else, that
a thimbleful of what
you'd been

would continue to exist.

If only you could rise
from death
as you once rose from sleep, as a child,

and walk through the rooms at night, fingering
the things
in the deep blue light, thinking, *Who*

was my mother before she was my mother, my

father, the clock? Ticking. The television, off.
But

this is the imagination's light. Outside,

the trees, anesthetized. And the stars
mass silently in the sky. They

said, *"Here are the maps";*
we burned the city. The people

are punishing the people—why?

THE THIGH

Clothing and weapons set aside, I am simply your thigh, and proof
that underneath the world lies
a warm pool of water overflowing
with drowned blue butterflies.

All these years,
clear up to here:
As you waited, I waited too.
When you were tired,
I lay down with you.
You never noticed,
but now you do. *(That
boy's fingers whispering past the hem of your skirt—guess who?)*

Guess who.

Sleeve of moony, vaporous voices. The dead ebbing as the living
        flowed.
The calm milked cows in a field of clover. The long
white fish in a bath. Cellular
shadow on the forest floor. Someone withdraws
a shining sword.
The naked man standing on the deck with his harpoon.
So much water lapping at a mindless shore. So
much spring stuffed into a pale
silk sack.
Or a club

tossed down among the flowers.

I am your memory
of it all, your life, in flesh and hours, statement
and tone, meat and weather

wrapped around a bone.

II.

THE PUNISHMENT

Spend a lifetime trying to trace
the veins of a maple leaf. Or

stare up into the dark
matter of space
and *your bad attitude*
floating

in lucid, invisible handfuls, chunks, and tons
above the garage: *Go*

out there and think about what you've done.

The seeds
sprouting, cells
dividing—take

a yardstick and measure
the length and width
of being, and then

translate it from inches
into centimeters.

O, moral and spiritual emptiness, *remember me.*
I will never be

such a girl again. From where

I stood in the world then, between

consciousness and nothing, selfhood
and infinity, thirteen, I could see

clearly, my parents' dream:
their single body cleaved,

finding itself whole

but imperfect again in me.

WAREHOUSE OF PRAYERS

1.

It's dark in here. Please, let me out.

2.

No, I hear him say. I want
to show you. And
to see it, you have to stay.

3.

And, O, I saw it then. So many prayers. Who
could answer them all? And yet

what god would have the heart to toss them out?

4.

Yes, he says, I know.
It terrifies.
The silence, and the din.
The tremendous weight of them. It defies

anything you might think
or say

about sound
about size.

But, yes, of course. Of course
I've kept them all.

5.

"We had gone for a walk in the dark.

Of all things, I was
deeply in love with my husband! Then

something silent
I couldn't see
crept out of the darkness,
and bit his hand."

6.

The beauty
of it. The great

beauty. The true
beauty of it. The beauty
beyond—

It's

bitten me. I'm
bleeding.

7.

In the dark one night you felt around
for your blue scarf. Its
blue diffusion. Its
shameless would-be sky.
But it was gone.

Gone, with your watch, and your wallet, and those
cheap beads. How

strange to understand, so suddenly

that none of it was yours. Not

a snippet, not a glimpse, not a bit, not

even the dust that had gathered

Amishly on it for years.

8.

And the green lawn rolls,
and the green lawn rolls
to the foot of it all,
to the foot of it all

telling the story of a world
created by a god,
who wanted to be loved
but did not like to talk.

9.

"We predicted this. Something

strapped to the chest of a child. Light
pouring up from holes in the ground. A fountain

run dry, and a mild-mannered man on a rampage in July.

Still, we were confused. We

thought we'd looked for this
trouble everywhere, and

never found a thing. We

believed there'd be more warning, despite
the many warnings. We

deeply believed a mistake had been made."

10.

Then, in the morning, a mannequin
sitting in the rain on the neighbor's porch. The rain
on the mannequin, like so many kisses
bestowed upon a corpse.

11.

No.
(He takes my hand. He opens a door.)

12.

Wow, I say.
So this is *all—*

and this is the vault in which they've hoarded it.

All:

What is, what was, what will be—

added to in increments. *(A skyful,
a pocketful, a teaspoonful, a pinch.)*

13.

And still, mostly vault.

14.

The blood
and the bed.
The basement full of blankets. The

freezer full of meat. *We*

all will rise again, and all be dignified.

The vein straight through the center

of the leaf.
The woody stem of a rose.
The dark suburban fruit of mulberries on the lawn.

We will rise over it all, and all of it will still
be here when we are gone.

15.

Hello. It's me, Eurydice. I want
to tell you about his eyes: Stupid

hopeful windows. *You*

idiot, I said.
All this resurrection business just
to have your dumb
love-glance sideswipe me dead.

16.

Her boy, in the war, the gate, left open, the field
full of flowers, the day, so cloudless, she couldn't help but see
the mysterious sense and emptiness of it:
As a child, he was so quiet, you could have drawn a circle

around it
with a piece of chalk.

You could have taken a bus to the edge of that silence, and
stepped off

onto a sidewalk, made of time, and walked

for years and years, all
through his childhood
and still kept walking.

17.

This
is the illegible scroll

on which Orpheus' reply was written.

This

is the book,
thrown from the window.

A cough.

A broken telephone.

A few notes of a song.

18.

And a woman sobbing in a hospital gown, *Not fair.*
Just this one body, and not even the body I wanted, and still
it clings to me weeping when I have to leave. Not fair.

19.

"Eurydice? Eurydice? Are you there?"

20.

RSVP: She

will not be arriving
by ship or by plane. No
car door slamming. No

driver to be paid. She
will not be walking. Neither shall she run.
Thank you for asking, but she can't come.

21.

Please, please, please, sweetheart,

pick up the fucking phone if you're there

22.

"The Czar was killed on the spot, as

were the Empress and the Grand Duchess Olga, neither
of whom could finish
making the sign of the cross.

But the daughters

wore corsets

lined with jewels. For
long moments the bullets,
fired at their chests,

ricocheted around the room."

23.

Please?

24.

One day I saw the divorcée take a letter from her ex-husband.
         Briefly, his
fingertips touched hers, and then she slipped the letter
into her purse:

But, O,
that purse,
full of old pleasure, and that letter. Memory, like a dark
hole full of feathers.

25.

"Lust, that goat in violets. Those
violets like so much tenderness

scattered in the grass. Love,

that rusty chain
dragging you home through your past."

26.

A woman turns at church in her pew and tells me before
the organ starts up, "I know
a story about your house."

27.

Oh? Yes?

28.

"In the forties, a farmer
named Elmer Barow,
in your kitchen, shot himself."

29.

Oh, I thought, *I know. I know.* Time,

passing, all along—the hum of the cobwebs in the corners
crocheting their intricate shrouds. The

dripping of the faucet. The
blackened toast. Of

course, when we sat down at the table with our heads bowed, that

was him listening in on our prayers—Elmer

Barow with a rifle in his mouth.

30.

Always
that

flash of desire,
always

in the way (that

gray cat sleeping
in the driveway, those

teenage girls bathing in a pond of bees)—that's

what's left of the freedom God
had to make us, or remain free.

31.

Eurydice?

32.

In winter a woman I work with gets the idea that her hands
are poisoned. She can't
touch anything anymore. She wears

gloves to bed, in case, in her sleep—

33.

No, E., of course your hands aren't poisoned. You
cannot kill your children if you stroke their hair. You

know this, you
know it.

34.

But, suddenly, gradually, myself—

everything I touch, there's—

35.

There's something wrong. (Not that. But
something.) I

spend hours trying not to think about the *something,* but it's

always there

in the shadowy tissue, in the silvery
microscopic gloom, the lazy
fluid slip of it, which,

released by love, billows
loosely around the cerebral cortex—

a poisoned flume.

36.

Then—?

37.

"And then the day is over, and the—"

38.

And the day is over.

And in the dark I hear God say,

Laura, go ahead and pray.

39.

Okay.

40.

Okay. I—
Okay. I—

Dear God, I—

offer up this prayer
of dryer lint and hair.

41.

Orpheus here
in a cellar made of glass.
In it, with me, a blizzard
of small black words. I

am sending this message
to you from the world, but
"This is a message from the world"
is all it says.

42.

"Oh, to the teeth, sweetness
is the medium, but the message
is decay. Like

the soul, a hunch, wrapped in disintegration. Sweater

wool, skin cells, carpet
fibers, ash, a gray

breeze: Virus,

and pollen, and ourselves

blown to breathing pieces."

43.

And then
at the petting zoo
I knew

animal terror
for the first time.
Animal

despair:
The trembling of the lamb
under my trembling hand.

44.

Suddenly, God
answers me!

I am made of the same thing you are, after all, and you

are made of me:

Some darkness, a supplication, a moral silence breezing

over the glassy stubble in a vacant field.

45.

"And let us not forget the petty prayers.
The insatiable hunger of seagulls. The sunset

in the blood, and those

birds turning

in on themselves,
crying, reeling, happiest
hungry. *Let us be*

your amphetamines! they scream. The market

full of fruit
out of season. The locked

door of the embassy. The high

gate surrounding spring:

Please, God, I want all of it for me."

46.

To: Orpheus
Fr: Eurydice
Re: Death

The babble. The cold, teeming, intangible hotel.

47.

God, do you hear that? That

bit of stitching in the wind? It
unravels when you listen.
Listen.

48.

The Debt Birds screeching, *Insufficient!*
Someone shoveling snow onto a fire.
A figure in a black suit swinging
a lantern through the dark

in arcs, coming
closer, and closer.

And my mother
standing by the lilac

(the lilac,
which is
the suburb's lyric poem

about death) talking

to a man she never met. I

overhear him say, Whatever

crazy sorrow saith.

49.

"No one was crying, no one was bleeding,
but the mail had been dumped in the street, and

someone's husband a few blocks over
was shouting loudly
about accountability.

Shadows stuffed into envelopes—as when
the forest creeps
to the edge of the freeway,
perfectly tamed,
finally revealed,

and the wild illegal animals
people keep as pets,

escape, are seen."

50.

Jesus Christ, this stuff is everywhere!

51.

Excuse me.

*I couldn't help
but overhear your prayer . . .*

52.

"What the bloody hell is this?
Someone must have written
down every word
ever said, then

shredded every word ever written."

53.

O, honey, O,
lovely, O,
please. It's
me,

Orpheus,
again,
Eurydice.

54.

"Okay, now
what we need here
is a warehouse,
or an abyss. Which
one of you guys
can get on this—

ASAP?"

55.

Like

trying to hold fire. Like

trying to hold perfume. Like

wearing fog to work. Like

stoppering a bottleful of light—

trying to talk to God.

56.

"Hello. Yeah. It's me Is he in? We've got a major mess on our
    hands."

57.

"Shit.
Shit.
Is he *ever* in?"

58.

Like
stoppering a bottleful of light. Like
wearing fog to work. Like
trying to hold perfume. Like

trying to hold fire—

to make the simplest goddamned contact with—

59.

O,
wait,
look
after all—that

warehouse, that

abyss, and

a beautiful naked stranger diligently trying

to ladle the oceans into it.

STROKE

The shadow
of the migration
on the ground

and a subtle girl with a rope.

This is the Styx, and the floodlight on the ferry, and the expressionless man with his pet jackal. The mattress strapped to your back. The bees and the scenery in your pot roast, mashed. The delicious shame of that. And the concentration. And desire. And your soul on a flagpole on the other side.

Where? Where?

It doesn't matter. They will take you only halfway there.

INTERRUPTION

Like a woman walking down the road with an armful of roses torn from her arms by an unexpected storm—long after you were gone, I just kept talking.

The tongue turned to shadow. A deer watched me carefully through a closed glass door. I grew younger and younger. I had accidents, like trysts. Sex, that whole last-ditch alphabet:

Kiss me screaming. Death completely forgot about me.

I just kept talking, long after you were gone. Long after the excavators had put down their tools to take a break, never to pick them up again. And the violinist had tossed his instrument into a ditch. And the ditch had filled with water. And the water had evaporated, revealing a whole orchestra of nothing but mud.

And then the path I'd worn—grew over with weeds. And the breeze, not whispering through the leaves in the trees. And finally something seemed to be saying to me:

Shut up, please,
and listen, Laura,
will you please listen to me?

AT GETTYSBURG

The one I love stands at the edge
of a wheatfield wearing
a blue cap, holding
a plastic musket in his hands. The one I love does a goofy

dance at Devil's Den. Mans a cannon. Waves
at me from a hill. He

dips his foot into Bloody Run. The sepia
dream of his dead body
is pulled by the water
over the rocks. And I

am the shadow of a stranger taking
his picture, laid out like so much black
drapery on the pavement. Is there

some better explanation? Was there

some other mossy, meandering
path we might have taken

to this place through time and space? Why

is it that where my heart
should be, there's
a small bright horse instead? While I

was simply standing
over there by a stone, waiting, did
an old woman run her bony
hand through my hair
and leave this gray ribbon there?

The one I love leans up against a fence, and then
pretends to be shot. He

opens his eyes
wide and grabs his chest, stumbles
backwards, falls
gracefully into the grass, where he lies

for a long time holding the sun in his arms. I take

another picture there. The worms
beneath him make

the burden of the earth seem light enough to bear—and still

inside me I believe I carry
the pond where the injured
swans have come to flock. I
believe I hold inside me
the lake into which the beautiful, armless
mortals wish to wade. I am

after all, their executioner and their creator, being
as I am, their mother. Were

they gods who came to earth to die and suffer, I wonder, or

boys who died and turned to gods? O,

the one I love needs sunblock, I think, too late, and,
perhaps, a bottle of water, but now

I have no idea where we are. *Where*

were you, God asks, *when I*
spread out the heavens and the earth? If you

were not there, then

how can you expect to know where you are now? Truly,

I don't know. I look around.
I say, *We're lost,*
to the one I love, who

looks over my shoulder and laughs. *No,*

Mom, he says
and points to dot and arrow
of ourselves on the map.

You're holding the battlefield upside down.

MISS BREVITY

I made the gown myself from minutes
held together with safety pins, and

wore it as I wafted through the nursery,
pouring light all over the crowns
of their heads. All

those ghostly babies in their rows. *O,*

you swear you'll remember us forever,
but you won't.

ELEGY

And now, it's all the same
to you—

the mouth, the sink, the dream.

A bed at the edge of an ocean's the same
as a train speeding
through Germany.

The Bureau of Travels
has approved all your plans, so you
no longer need

your passport, your cell phone, your coat

to blaze screaming
through the vast North, waving

a flag on fire in the snowy forest, pouring

wine all over the ground, draping
the rearview mirrors
of my car
with red cloth, fogging

the windows, locking the doors, staging

all this silence and emptiness and rust
to torment me, to reveal to me
the hidden mechanics
of lust, having

graduated,
as you did this morning, from being
a humble student of the universe

to its greatest authority.

III.

MISS ESTROGEN

To have been a storm in a suit of armor. (Or the hound

tied up outside
as the fox slipped quivering through the field.) To have been

fever in an envelope
mailed to a fire (while

a man in the bedroom shouted, having

mortally wounded himself
while sharpening his own knife.) Like

unpredictable furniture
for many years. *(She
has her period, she's madly in love, leave
her alone, she's out of her mind.)* Or like

a red carpet rolled through a forest, ending at an ocean.
(What

will become of your life
without such desire?) To have been

the wind in the kitchen, which blew
the plates and bowls from the cupboards, as the oven

door lolled open. Or a dormouse
in a wineglass. Such
sacred fury. (Was it meaningless?) Pageant

in a matchbox. All
the mirrors and tiaras locked up in a vault, as I

scaled, in my satin robe, the prison walls, ran
straight into the burning church in my burning stilettos.
(And then

so many bewildered, dusty knickknacks on a shelf.

For Sale: *Curios.*
Everything must go.)

Once, someone
nodded in my direction as I did my job. "She's

the temporary girl here"—meaning me. Once

someone pointed and said, "Look
at that wild bird in that tree."

I looked
too late. It had flown away.
To have been

that bird, and to become that tree.

MY FATHER'S FEET

They are thoughts, on earth, in shoes, stepping
slowly over the layers of leaf
and heaven decomposing.

He was a mailman for twenty years. Twenty
miles a day through rain and . . .

The hedges between one day
and the next, one
day and our deaths, were dark

but immaterial. My father
walked straight through them, shod

in diligence, without

self-knowledge, or pretense,

and without stumbling. He

suffered, but did not question. He
rowed his lotus boats down that river in no
particular direction, this

world growing heavier as he carried it, and still,

he plods on.

My father, my first
and only messenger of God.

THE BAD TEACHER

She could come to the door in September for our son.

All thistled cursive and miscounted nickels. She
might tell him facts he'll recall all his life:

Mice are spontaneously
generated by garbage.
The size of the skull is the size of the mind.
At the end of all this love
and fuss, we die. *Everything
your mother told you about eternity was a lie.*

I imagine her at night at a desk made for a child.
Her knees too high. Her elbows
rest on the floor. Switched

off for summer. An awful
doll. *(I should have burned her as a girl, this has gone too far.)*
Her spine and her eyes have been
sewn closed
by the same seamstress
who sewed this:

a black felt scrap of nightmare, its
edges stitched up sloppily to the stars.

MISS WEARINESS

At first she looked like all the other girls, but then

the chipped fingernail, and then

she sat down in a folding chair
and let the other girls pass by

in their ballgowns, in their bathing suits, in their
beatific smiles, but she

had tossed her heels aside.

Enough of industry, enough
of goals and troubles, looking ahead, grooming, and dreaming
and anything that ended
in *i-n-g* in this
life ever again, she said.

O, enough, even, of the simple stuff:

The will-'o-the-wisp, the rain on a lake, all
those goldfish in their plastic
baggies at the fair. To them

it must have been
as if the world were divided
into small warped dreams, nowhere

to get to, and nothing to do but swim.

PRAYER

Weren't we out of milk? And the cheese? Did we not eat the cheese? The bread? Certainly that plastic bag was empty, maybe one stale piece. So how did it become this endlessness of bread? Whence came the dozen eggs, the whales and ravens, the herd of deer poured down the hillside, the bloody cardboard carton of eternal raspberries?

And why do such miracles and mysteries terrify me? The secret file in some hive-like office complex—our name and address tucked away. The beautiful suffering animals painted on the ancient walls of a cave. The ship's wake streaming from one shore to the other. Not just my family, the whole hungry country. *The species.* The children praying at an altar. The brakes of a truck screeching. The sun rising on a field of wheat. The sudden groceries. And, over it all, the spirit, like a snowy owl.

The eye of a sparrow, blinking.
The floating, and the falling.
The soundless waves of sad ecstatic memories.
Such freedom, such need.

MANNA

And what might it taste like? Think

clotted oxygen. Permanent snow. So

many spongy stones, each
containing at its center
the last earthly word of a ghost.

Think of the flesh on an angel's hips, pinched
into morsels. Candied soap. Small
lozenges of condensed foam.
Six seconds of bliss, rolled
in powdered sugar, deep-
fried, rolled again in the white
blood cells of a child,

then left in the shade to multiply.

Yes.
Solid fluff.
Weighted hopes.
Pale
lumps of fresh
heaven, like
some type of old-fashioned candy
your grandmother always remembered
from childhood, and then

searched for all her life,
never found again, but never
ceased to desire: You

find one of those in your pocket
a few days after she dies.

HAG

I saw her once
when I was very young—an old

woman with a melted face. She

was standing in the doorway
to my bedroom,
and when I screamed, she walked away.

Suppose

the beauty of the moon
could be held against you? Suppose

the air always smelled
exactly this way—all

the flowers of spring on the breeze
caught in a wine skin, the wine having been

spilled freely
as you laughed about its spilling
years and years before? *Listen,*

the way

we wasted those days

on that green lawn—

the way our friends—

and the way—

and the way the graves—

and the way—

Yes. And the horses
faltered during the parade.
And the couple making love
on a blanket in the sun
were in the process of becoming
a thing with one bald wing between them.
And then

a small boy running through a forest
carrying in his hands
a red-hot coal, while,
overhead, a bird flew south, and

in its beak, a bit of your soul.

And then, of course, all
the tangible, divine just-loosened
hair of nuns
spiraling toward you, and all
the uncontrolled laughter of twelve year-olds, all
the hydroelectric power of the Atlantic seacoast
in you, all

the songs written on envelopes
accidentally tossed
onto raging fires.

And the winning
lottery tickets. And the flippant
remarks of sorority sisters. And

the wedding dresses stuffed into dumpsters:

It threw off sparks.
It lit up the abyss.

Once, it was of you,

and you were of it. O,

imagine, you
were a middle-aged woman once
at the supermarket with a secret. That

secret was like supernal light, like
light flowing peacefully
back to its source, speaking

French, made of pleasure. And you

disdained no creature. You loved them all. You
threw the fish you caught back into the water. You
walked your neighbor's dog. And,

all that time, the ocean churning
all that reluctance
out as it churned.

You never even heard
the halfhearted warning
of the woodpecker tapping its bill
on the roof of your house as it burned. Yes,

you decided, you

would live forever if they let you, like
a snail at the equator setting out that very day
to make a silvery circle around the world
by standing still as it turned.

And the way—

And the way—

One season tossed

sloppily onto another. Tomorrow
you said, you'd

write those thank-you notes. Tomorrow
you'd call it off with your lover.

But tomorrow you ran through the sprinklers
on the courthouse lawn instead, because
tomorrow you could be dead. O,

your life, so long, it became

a lovely punishment made
of pale blue feathers and cashmere sweaters.

And the way—

And the way—

The fluorescent silence of a coral reef
dying under the sea.

To find yourself
finally
lingering in a doorway:

A woman with a question,
and moss in her hair, who, when she
leaned in to say to her younger self, *It's me,*

simply turned quietly away
when I began to scream.

WAR WITH TOY SOLDIERS

They have fallen off the coffee table
onto the floor. They have slipped
under rugs, lost
their guns, found

themselves in the strange
gray dream between
the floral cushions and the upholstery. They

have been batted all over the house by the cat, dropped
their canteens
down the register grates, forgotten

their homelands, their languages, their names. They

have fallen out of love.
Boarded the wrong trains.
Laughed loud and long late into the night
while digging their own graves. They

have bathed in rain. Trudged through mud. Been
drunk. Driven

in long convoys of trucks without brakes across desert plains.

They have stood at the edges
of swiftly moving rivers, watching

time flounder down to the ocean, singing,
Once, there was not even a plan.
A plan still had to be made.

Now, it's Monday. September.
The children have vanished
from the dream of their summer vacation, and

a mother, on her knees, alone
in the house for the first time in months
could assess this situation, could see

how the pure white deer that always wanders

onto the battlefield
after the violence

stands now at the center
of the wonder in silence.

MISS POST-APOCALYPSE

The shoes in the garden seemed
to know me by my name. Emptied, all of them, except

for the whispering of the breeze as it blew
over that emptiness and loosened
their tongues: *Girl,*
where

are all your trashy little daydreams now? (O,

my face on the page of a magazine
curled up in the fire. Me, smiling
on a big TV worshiping
a box of Tide.)

I couldn't bring myself to walk
home beneath that monstrous
cloud. I went

back to the factory instead.

I walked for miles.
But the gate was locked.
From somewhere inside,
I could hear

the last man on earth
curse the last

card as he drew it from the deck.

WELCOME WAGON

O, it only seems
we've never met before. This
cool well from which you draw
your daily cup
has caused you to forget. We

were strangers
in your dreams. Passengers
on delayed flights. Gardeners,
glimpsed from passing trains. We
were on our knees. We

were flowergirls, painted
by Impressionists. Boys
you passed on the beach. We'd

been fishing. We were carrying
our heavy buckets full of fish and blood, happily.

Or, you saw us briefly in magazines, flipping
the pages fast. A pregnant

woman stepping
carefully out of her bath. A child,
barefoot, riding
a donkey through still water. We were

the excavators, lying
in the sun beside our tools
as you jogged by. The teenage girl sulking
beside her mother at the mall. In death

you clawed us up
through the lacerated
satin, hauled

us from the lake
with a chain, waving
away the silver

flies on our faces, surprised

to find we'd been here all along, waiting

for you on the other
side of yourself

in our nameless patience.

MISS CONSOLATION FOR EMOTIONAL DAMAGES

When the embarrassment began, no one could see it. It lived

in the closet, the basement, the attic, the brain. It was
a moth at first, and then it was the hole a moth had made.

It had to do with unemployment: No! (Who
cared that my father couldn't work?) It had

to do with the boy next door, who'd
seen my mother drunk, whose
own mother had explained to him
that it wasn't our fault we were poor.

No.

It had been born
in another country. It had come to this one on a boat.
It couldn't speak the language. It had
left a wolf
on the other shore. (A tame
wolf: someone
had beaten the wildness out of it
with kindness, and a stick.) It had

to do with paradox, that space was transparent
and also dense.
It had to do with Einstein.
The curvature of the world in a third dimension. It couldn't

take the contradiction, woke
one morning as a careless
American girl, mouth
stuffed with pink
fluff: When

she opened it, for centuries, nothing
but pleasant inanities came out.

UNTITLED

In the library, a book
written in a voice made out of dust
waiting on a shelf
covered with dust.

The pop machine
is out of order.
The drinking
fountain has run dry. But

thirst is what we're here for, driving
everything we do, inspiring
every word we utter. The couches

are crowded
with the dozing homeless, from

whom the world's dreams rise as titles in dusty light . . .

Unsolved Murders. Middlemarch. The Wild Swans at Coole. My

whole life has been a lie:

A lie made out of substance
—*butter mixed with dust.*

A lie you could mold
with your hands.

But a good lie, a lie
worthy of a life.

MY FATHER'S CLOSET

The birdlessness of a winter night is in it. The phantom lover writing letters on the wind.

Well, Laura, you always wanted a sailboat, didn't you? You wanted an aeolian harp. You wanted a white room filled with white flowers. Well, here it is. Here we sit, waiting for a woman wounded with light to call us in. This is your father's name on her lips. This is the village into which we've slipped. In the night. Via pills. With cataracts, aneurysms, fractured hips. That little apprehension? Yes. This was it. The subliminal message in the mist at the edges of the screen? All those years, all that peace, you could barely repress this scream.

Listen: A chorus a million miles away is singing *Solace, solaced, don't be ridiculous.*

The only suit my father ever owned is in it. The psyche's anchor sunk deep in an ocean of thoughtlessness. A child brooding over her own origins, making crystals in a dish—in it. All the plans of animals—their blueprints and files, the envelopes on which they scrawled their desperate grocery lists:

A silence follows it.
A silence preceded it.
This was it.
This is it.

NEW DRESS (3)

A small bird flapped its wings
crazily over me. *How*

did it get in here? I asked
the security guard. He
said, *Don't ask me.*

Together, we watched it for a while. It was
no longer spring. Not
even summer. It was fall. But I'd

come to buy a spring dress at the mall.

I don't know, he said.
I don't know, watching
that bird circle the brilliant
emptiness over us, chirping. *Maybe*

it likes it here. He shrugged. *It's safe. It's clean.*

He wasn't a young
man. He had a uniform, but no
badge, no gun. He

startled when a girl
squealed in the food court, and I
briefly considered
touching his hand
but then thought better of it. *(Who*

needs a dress at all

in this resplendent pall?) He

told me he'd once seen

an injured hawk being
dragged down a river
to its death. *All*

these years, he said, *I've wondered why
I didn't save it, didn't
even try.* If I'd

been less shy
I might have told him
that it seemed to me this thing he'd seen
had been the physical
manifestation
of passing time,

and that was why. But I

told him instead that I'd once stood
on the street
outside a library
and watched a pigeon
fluster on a gargoyle. When

the pigeon flew away, the gargoyle

also seemed to fly, and that
flying nothing seemed to cast

a shadow on the ground. It

still embarrassed me, I
confessed to him, to remember

the way I'd screamed, seeing

that shadow
of nothing,
on a busy street.

Yeah, he said

after a long silence. He
remembered that. He'd
been there, too, he believed,
beside me, also screaming.

ACKNOWLEDGMENTS

Some of these poems have been published or are forthcoming in *The American Poetry Review, The Colorado Review, Gulf Coast, The Iowa Review, Lake Effect, The Laurel Review, The New England Review, The New Republic, Pleiades, Poetry,* and *Salt Hill.* "At Gettysburg" was republished in *Best American Poetry 2006.* A fellowship from the National Endowment of the Arts supported the completion of this collection.

Ausable Press is grateful to

The New York State Council on the Arts

The National Endowment for the Arts

The New York Community Trust

for their generous support.

CPSIA information can be obtained
at www.ICGtesting.com
Printed in the USA
OW12s0925210317
941LV00001B/2/P